I Have a Secret

AUTHOR'S NOTE

This is a message for the child reading this book.

   If you are a child who has had something bad happen to you, something bad you have felt you have to keep secret, I'm sorry. That should not have happened. You are not alone. Bad things happen too often to too many people. It is a sad part of life in this world.

   A bad thing happened to the child in this book. If you are a child who has had a bad thing happen to you, you might see yourself in his story. This is why he is sharing his story.

   If you are a child who has not had a bad thing happen that you had to keep secret, I am glad. You should know that reading this book could still be difficult.

   As the author of this book, I want to apologize if this book makes you feel sad. I also want to apologize if this book makes you remember something that happened to you that you would rather forget or not think about. I want to apologize if this book makes you feel angry. Those are not fun things to feel or think about.

I do believe that those feelings and thoughts are important. Stories of pain are important. Stories where bad things happen are important to read because bad things do happen, and I believe that if more stories about people who had bad things happen to them are told, those bad things will happen less.

Thank you for reading. If after reading this introduction, you have decided you do not want to read this book, I more than understand. You are not being a coward, you are taking care of yourself, and no one knows what you need better than you, and don't let me or anyone else tell you otherwise.

Andrew Barnett

I Have a Secret

Andrew Barnett
Illustrator: Andrea Fietta

Grateful Steps
Asheville, North Carolina

Grateful Steps Foundation, 30 Ben Lippen School Road #107, Asheville, North Carolina 28806; Copyright © 2020 by Andrew Barnett. Barnett, Andrew; *I Have a Secret;* Illustrator Andrea Fietta; ISBN 978-1-945714-43-6 Paperback. Printed in the United States of America at Lightning Source; FIRST EDITION. All rights reserved. No part of this book may be reproduced in any manner whatsoever without written permission from the author. www.gratefulsteps.org

I am a child, and there is something happening to me that I feel worried about.

I have a problem.

It is a problem I hope isn't happening to anyone else in the whole world, but I bet there are other people out there who are dealing with this too.

**There is someone I know who does things to me
I don't like, and I want that person to stop.**

**I know that person shouldn't be doing these bad things
and would get in trouble if anyone found out
about what they are doing to me.**

**I want these bad things to STOP,
but I don't want that person to get in trouble.**

This person cares about me, or at least says so.

This person also told me not to tell anyone about this.

If this person gets in trouble, I feel it would be my fault, and then I am afraid of what might be said or done to me after it's learned that I was the one who caused the trouble in the first place.

I have not told anyone about the bad things
this person does to me.

I haven't even told you what this bad thing is.
I am scared to tell. I am also scared not to tell
because then this bad thing will keep happening.

I feel stuck, like there is not a good solution
to this problem, and I don't know what to do.

I am carrying this very big secret by myself, and I don't like carrying a big secret like this.

It does not feel good.

Sometimes, I feel there are others who already know the secret, and they are going to tell other people, and this worries me a lot.

There are times I feel other people can read inside my mind and know I have a secret. It can feel as if this secret is written in marker on my face for everyone to see.

Sometimes, I am thinking about the thing
that no one else should know,
and I can't stop thinking about it,
and I am scared I am going to tell someone.

Tell secret

Keep secret

Having a secret is hard and makes me feel bad.

What is happening to me also makes me feel bad.

Adults are supposed to help you feel safe.

Adults are supposed to take care of you.

Adults are not supposed to hit you.

They are also not supposed to touch you
or poke you in your private places.

Adults are not supposed to do things like that.

But some adults do things like that,
and some do things like that to children.

There is someone who does things like that to me.

I am not going to tell you what my secret is.

I don't know you. Because I don't know you, it is hard for me to know I can trust you. Even if you are a trustworthy person, I am not going to tell you my secret right now.

There are some people I do know and trust. There are some adults I know and trust.

I want to find the courage to tell them. I am also very scared. I am scared that if I tell someone, something bad will happen to me.

I am also scared that something bad could happen to the person who is doing the thing to me that I have felt I have to keep secret.

It is my choice whether or not I tell someone.
It is always my choice. I own my secrets.

Keeping a secret inside hurts,
but I can choose to do it.

But maybe I don't want to keep it inside anymore.

Maybe I don't like keeping this secret.

Maybe I want the bad things that have
been happening to me to stop happening.

As soon as this book is over, I think
I am going to go tell someone my secret
about the bad things that happen to me.

It is hard for me to trust that
everything is going to be okay,
and I wish I did not have to deal with this.

I can deal with this. I have been dealing with this.
I am strong. I can tell my secret.

This is my choice. I did not choose to have something bad happen to me.

I can choose to tell someone.

AFTERWORD

This is a message for adults and children. It is written to make some things about this book clearer.

Telling someone about abuse of any kind can go a number of different ways.

The person you tell might believe you.

The person you tell might not believe you.

The person you tell might do whatever they can to support you.

The person you tell might be mad at you for telling them.

The person you tell might tell you they love you and respect you and will do what they can to protect you.

The person you tell might blame you for what happened to you.

Telling someone might make the problem better.

Telling someone might make the problem worse.

There is no magic cure for something as terrible as the abuse of a child.

There are no magic words to make it better.

There is no way to erase the past.

This book wants you to feel that you are not alone and that there are people out there who care.

And if you do choose to tell someone about your pain, this book is proud of you.

And if you choose to keep your pain a secret for now, this book respects you.

Included in this book is a list of resources—for children and parents—to assist on the healing journey.

RESOURCE LIST:

Childhelp

Website: childhelp.org

Phone number: 1-800-422-4453

Childhelp runs the National Child Abuse Hotline, which is also available anytime. They can assist in reporting instances of child abuse, as well as provide individualized resources and support to help with issues of abuse.

Darkness to Light

Wesbite: www.d2l.org

Phone number: 1-866-FOR-LIGHT
or text 'LIGHT' to 741741

24 hr. Call line with licensed counselors for resources and support regarding the sexual abuse of a child. Also provides opportunities for training and additional resources for helping loved ones who have been victims of abuse.

RAINN

Website: rainn.org

Phone number: 1-800-656-4673

Provides resources for victims of sexual abuse and assualt and their loved ones, including a crisis line and an online chat to receive individualized care and support.